**Also by the same author,
and available in Coronet Books:**

You're a Winner, Charlie Brown (1)
For the Love of Peanuts (2)
Good Ol' Snoopy (3)
Who do you think you are, Charlie Brown (4)
Fun with Peanuts (5)
Here Comes Snoopy (6)
You're my Hero, Charlie Brown (7)
This is Your Life, Charlie Brown (8)
Let's Face It, Charlie Brown (9)
Slide! Charlie Brown, Slide! (10)
All This and Snoopy, Too (11)
Good Grief, Charlie Brown! (12)
Here's To You, Charlie Brown (13)
Nobody's Perfect Charlie Brown (14)
Very Funny, Charlie Brown (15)
We're On Your Side, Charlie Brown! (16)
Hey, Peanuts (17)
You're a Brave Man Charlie Brown (18)
We Love You, Snoopy (19)
Peanuts for Everybody (20)
You're Too Much, Charlie Brown (21)
Here Comes Charlie Brown (22)
You've Done It Again, Charlie Brown (23)
The Wonderful World of Peanuts (24)
Charlie Brown and Snoopy (25)
What Next, Charlie Brown (26)
You're the Greatest, Charlie Brown (27)
It's For You Snoopy (28)
Have It Your Way, Charlie Brown (29)
You're Not For Real Snoopy (30)
What Now Charlie Brown (32)
You're Something Special, Snoopy (33)
You've Got A Friend, Charlie Brown (34)
Take It Easy, Charlie Brown (35)

Knight Books
Don't Tread On Charlie Brown
Meet The Peanuts Gang
What Were You Saying Charlie Brown

Film Special
A Boy Named Charlie Brown

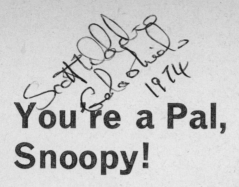

You're a Pal, Snoopy!

Selected Cartoons from YOU NEED HELP,
CHARLIE BROWN, Vol. 2

Charles M. Schulz

CORONET BOOKS
Hodder Fawcett Ltd., London

Copyright © 1964, 1965 by United Feature
Syndicate, Inc.
First published 1972 by Fawcett Publications Inc.,
New York
Coronet edition 1972
Second impression 1973
Third impression 1973

Printed and bound in Great Britain for
Coronet Books,
Hodder Fawcett Ltd,
St. Paul's House, Warwick Lane,
London, EC4P 4AH
by Hazell Watson & Viney Ltd,
Aylesbury, Bucks

ISBN 0 340 15696 1

HERE, NOW! YOU TWO STOP THAT FIGHTING! STOP IT, I SAY!
SLURP! SLURP! SLURP!
WHO'S FIGHTING? I SURRENDER!
I SAID, I SURRENDER! STOP IT! I SURRENDER! I SURRENDER!
I SAID, I SURRENDER!!!
SCHULZ

I WONDER IF THERE ARE "PEOPLE" STARS AND "DOG" STARS?

SCHULZ

ALL THIS AND SNOOPY TOO - FROM CORONET

Peanuts
CHARLES M. SCHULZ

☐	02709 6	You're a Winner, Charlie Brown (1)	25p
☐	02710 X	For the Love of Peanuts (2)	25p
☐	04491 8	Good Ol' Snoopy (3)	25p
☐	04409 8	Who do you think you are, Charlie Brown (4)	25p
☐	04305 9	Fun with Peanuts (5)	25p
☐	04295 8	Here Comes Snoopy (6)	25p
☐	04318 0	You're my Hero, Charlie Brown (7)	25p
☐	04406 3	This is Your Life, Charlie Brown (8)	25p
☐	04294 X	Let's Face It, Charlie Brown (9)	25p
☐	04407 1	Slide! Charlie Brown, Slide! (10)	25p
☐	04405 5	All This and Snoopy, Too (11)	25p
☐	10788 X	Good Grief, Charlie Brown! (12)	25p
☐	10595 X	Here's To You, Charlie Brown (13)	25p
☐	10541 0	Nobody's Perfect Charlie Brown (14)	25p
☐	10673 5	Very Funny, Charlie Brown (15)	25p
☐	10760 X	We're On Your Side, Charlie Brown! (16)	25p
☐	10761 8	Hey, Peanuts (17)	25p
☐	12838 0	You're a Brave Man Charlie Brown (18)	25p
☐	12786 4	We Love You, Snoopy (19)	25p
☐	12609 4	Peanuts for Everybody (20)	25p
☐	12614 0	You're Too Much, Charlie Brown (21)	25p
☐	12618 3	Here Comes Charlie Brown (22)	25p
☐	12521 7	You've Done It Again, Charlie Brown (23)	25p
☐	12543 8	The Wonderful World of Peanuts (24)	25p
☐	12520 9	Charlie Brown and Snoopy (25)	25p
☐	12544 6	What Next, Charlie Brown (26)	25p
☐	15135 8	You're the Greatest, Charlie Brown (27)	25p
☐	15829 8	It's For You Snoopy (28)	25p
☐	15828 X	Have It Your Way, Charlie Brown (29)	20p
☐	15698 8	You're Not For Real Snoopy (30)	25p
☐	16712 2	What Now Charlie Brown (32)	25p
☐	17322 X	You're Something Special, Snoopy (33)	25p
☐	17417 X	You've Got A Friend, Charlie Brown (34)	25p
☐	17844 2	Take It Easy, Charlie Brown (35)	25p

Knight Books

☐ 04234	6	Don't Tread On Charlie Brown	20p
☐ 10660	3	Meet The Peanuts Gang	20p
☐ 14804	7	What Were You Saying Charlie Brown	20p

Film Special

☐ 13476	3	A Boy Named Charlie Brown	90p

JOHNNY HART

☐ 15694	5	Hey! B.C.	25p
☐ 15679	1	B.C. Strikes Back	25p
☐ 16477	8	Back To B.C.	25p
☐ 16879	X	Hurray For B.C.	25p
☐ 16881	1	What's New B.C.?	25p

JOHNNY HART & BRANT PARKER

☐ 15816	6	The King is a Fink	25p
☐ 15812	2	The Wondrous Wizard of Id	25p
☐ 16476	X	The Peasants Are Revolting	25p
☐ 16899	4	Remember The Golden Rule	25p

GOSCINNY and UDERZO

☐ 16054	3	Asterix the Gaul	25p
☐ 16053	5	Asterix in Britain	25p
☐ 16807	2	Asterix and Cleopatra	25p

ERIC THOMSON

☐ 15543	4	The Adventures of Dougal	25p
☐ 15544	2	Dougal's Scottish Holiday	25p

All these books are available at your bookshop or newsagent, or can be ordered direct from the publisher. Just tick the titles you want and fill in the form below.

CORONET BOOKS, P.O. Box 11, Falmouth, Cornwall.

Please send cheque or postal order. No currency, and allow the following for postage and packing:

1 book – 7p per copy, 2–4 books – 5p per copy, 5–8 books – 4p per copy, 9–15 books – 2½p per copy, 16–30 books – 2p per copy in U.K., 7p per copy overseas.

Name...

Address...